KS1
4–6
Years

Master Maths at Home

Measuring

Scan the QR code to help your child's learning at home.

 DK |  **MATHS NO PROBLEM!**

mastermathsathome.com

How to use this book

Maths — No Problem! created **Master Maths at Home** to help children develop fluency in the subject and a rich understanding of core concepts.

Key features of the Master Maths at Home books include:

- Carefully designed lessons that provide structure, but also allow flexibility in how they're used. For example, some children may want to write numbers, while others might want to trace.

- Speech bubbles containing content designed to spark diverse conversations, with many discussion points that don't have obvious 'right' or 'wrong' answers.

- Rich illustrations that will guide children to a discussion of shapes and units of measurement, allowing them to make connections to the wider world around them.

- Exercises that allow a flexible approach and can be adapted to suit any child's cognitive or functional ability.

- Clearly laid-out pages that encourage children to practise a range of higher-order skills.

- A community of friendly and relatable characters who introduce each lesson and come along as your child progresses through the series.

You can see more guidance on how to use these books at **mastermathsathome.com**.

We're excited to share all the ways you can learn maths!

Copyright © 2022 Maths — No Problem!

Maths — No Problem!
mastermathsathome.com
www.mathsnoproblem.com
hello@mathsnoproblem.com

First published in Great Britain in 2022 by
Dorling Kindersley Limited
One Embassy Gardens, 8 Viaduct Gardens, London SW11 7BW
A Penguin Random House Company

The authorised representative in the EEA is Dorling Kindersley
Verlag GmbH. Amulfstr. 124, 80636 Munich, Germany

10 9 8 7 6 5 4 3 2
003–327067–Jan/22

A CIP catalogue record for this book is available from the British Library.

ISBN: 978-0-24153-908-8
Printed and bound in the UK

For the curious
www.dk.com

This book was made with Forest Stewardship Council™ certified paper - one small step in DK's commitment to a sustainable future. For more information go to www. dk.com/our-green-pledge

Acknowledgements
The publisher would like to thank the authors and consultants Andy Psarianos, Judy Hornigold, Adam Gifford and Dr Anne Hermanson.

The Castledown typeface has been used with permission from the Colophon Foundry.

Contents

Ruby   Elliott   Amira   Charles   Lulu   Sam   Oak   Holly   Ravi   Emma   Jacob   Hannah

Comparing the heights of objects

Starter

How can we compare the towers?

Example

 is the **tallest**.

It is **taller** than and .

 is the **shortest**.

It is **shorter** than and .

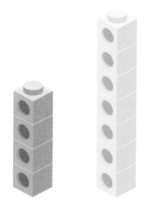

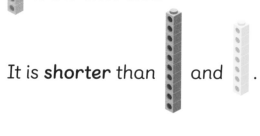

We can put the towers in order from shortest to tallest.

A   B   C

(a) Compare the houses using **taller** and **shorter**.

 is [ ] than .

 is [ ] than .

(b) Put the houses in order from tallest to shortest.

[ ] , [ ] , [ ]

Tree A   Tree B   Tree C   Tree D

Compare the trees using **taller** or **shorter**.

(a) Tree A is [ ] than Tree B.

(b) Tree C is [ ] than Tree A.

(c) Tree B is [ ] than Tree D.

(d) Tree D is [ ] than trees A, B and C.

(e) Tree C is [ ] than trees A, B and D.

Comparing the lengths of objects

Jacob lined up crayons on a page in his book.

How can we compare the crayons?

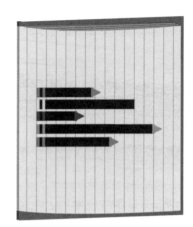

Example

The crayons are not all the same length.

The crayons have different lengths.

is the **longest**.

is the **shortest**.

Longest means longer than any of the others.

We can order the crayons from longest to shortest.

1 Circle the item that is the **longest**.

(a)

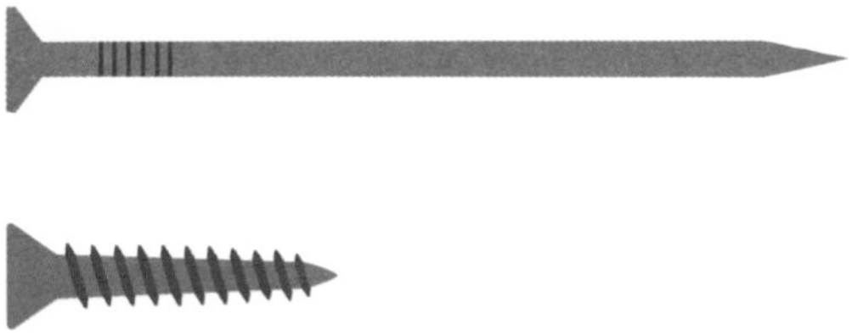

(b)

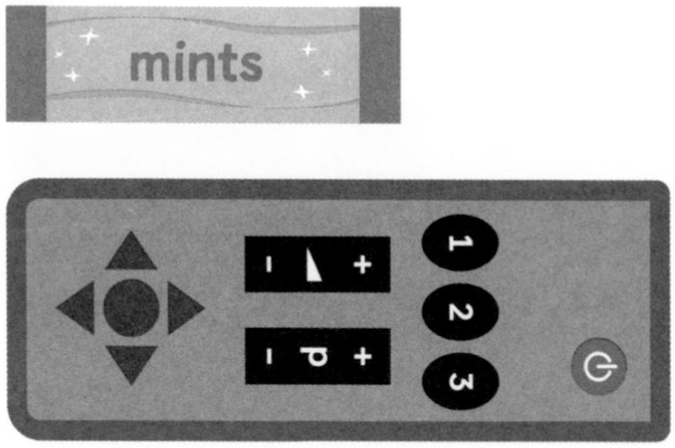

mints

2 Circle the item that is the **shortest**.

(a)

(b)

3 Order the **mints**, the **screw** and the **watch** from shortest to longest.

mints

, ,

shortest → longest

Using objects to measure length and height

Starter

Which pencil case is longer? How can we tell?

Example

We can use objects to help us measure.

I am using ☐ .

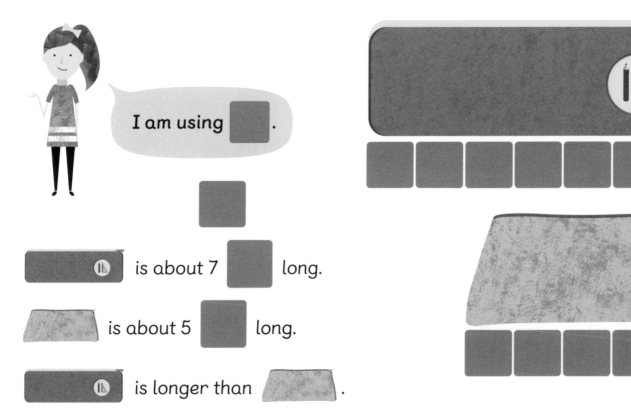

☐ is about 7 ☐ long.

☐ is about 5 ☐ long.

☐ is longer than ☐ .

We can use objects to measure height.

The soldier is about the same height as four tiles.

Practice

1

Fill in the blanks.

(a) ━━━━ is about [ ] tiles long.

(b) ━━━━━ is about [ ] tiles long.

(c) ━━━━ is [ ] than ━━ .

2

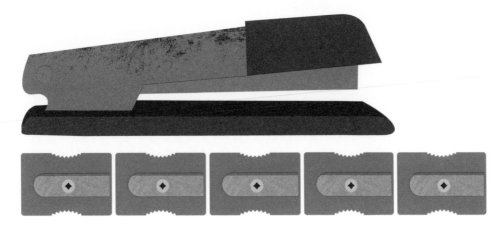

The stapler is about pencil sharpeners long.

Using body parts to measure length and height

Starter

How tall is the plant?

Example

You can measure with hands. The plant is about 10 hands tall.

If we use the length of our hand, the plant is about 5 hands tall.

What if we used the length of our hand? Would the plant still be about 10 hands tall?

We can say that one hand is 1 unit of measure.

I am going to use my foot as a unit of measure.

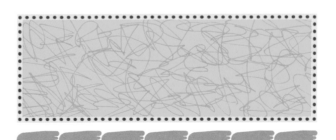

The rug is about the length of 7 feet. It is about 7 units long.

1   Count the ✋ .

The 🪑 is about ⬜ hands tall.

One ✋ is 1 unit.

The height of the chair is about ⬜ units.

2   Measure your  using the length of your ✊ as a unit.

My bed is about ⬜ ✊ long.

3   Measure your  using the length of your ✋ as a unit.

My bed is about ⬜ ✋ long.

Using a ruler to measure length and height

How long is the pen?

How tall is the mug?

Example

We can use a ruler to measure objects.

The pen measures 10 cm. It is 10 cm long.

Line up one end of the object with 0 cm on the ruler.

The mug measures 8 cm.
It is 8 cm tall.

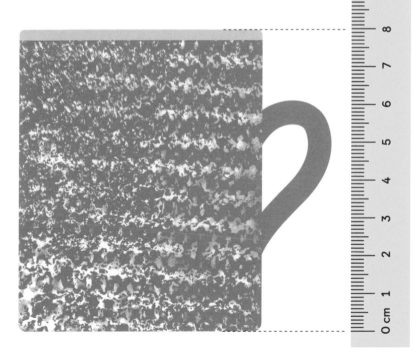

1 Use a ruler to measure these lines.

(a)

☐ cm

(b)

☐ cm

(c)

☐ cm

(d)

☐ cm

2 Use a ruler to measure the length of these objects.

(a) 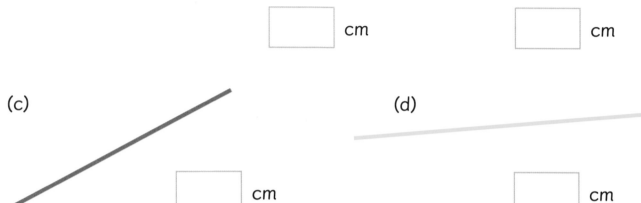 ☐ cm

(b) ☐ cm

3 Use a ruler to measure the length or height of some of your favourite toys. Record your results here.

Toy	Length or height	cm
teddy		

Using next, before and after

Charles is making a sandwich.
How can we describe what he does?

> We can use **next**, **before** and **after** to describe the order of things.

Before Charles makes a sandwich, he washes his hands.

Next, he takes two slices of bread.

Next, he puts the cheese and the tomato onto one slice of bread.

Next, he puts the other slice of bread on top.

After he makes the sandwich, he sits down to eat it.

1 This is what Ravi did yesterday evening.

first	second	third	fourth

played with toys   read a story   watched TV   went to bed

(a) What did Ravi do before he read a story?

(b) What did Ravi do after he watched TV?

(c) Ravi played with his toys at 5 o'clock in the afternoon.
    What did he do next?

2 Circle the correct words.

(a) Ravi played with his toys **before/after** he watched TV.

(b) Ravi went to bed **after/before** he read a story.

(c) Ravi read a story, then he **watched TV/went to bed**.

Telling time to the hour

Starter

What time does the clock show?

Example

The minute hand is longer than the hour hand.

→ The minute hand shows us the minutes.

→ The hour hand shows us the hour.

→ This is the minute hand.

→ This is the hour hand.

The hour hand is pointing to 2. The minute hand is on 12.

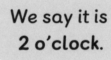

We say it is 2 o'clock.

The time is 2 o'clock.

1 Write the time for each clock.

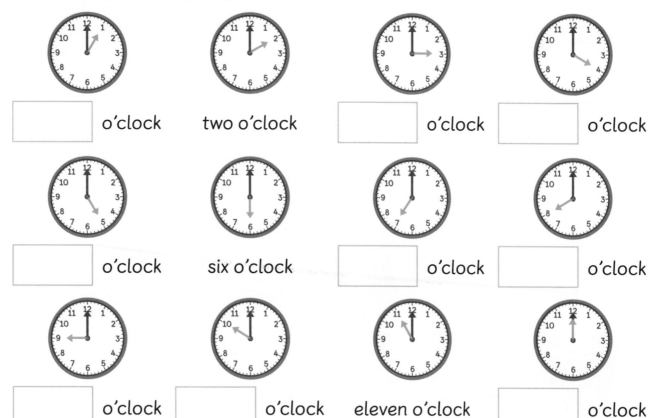

[   ] o'clock   two o'clock   [   ] o'clock   [   ] o'clock

[   ] o'clock   six o'clock   [   ] o'clock   [   ] o'clock

[   ] o'clock   [   ] o'clock   eleven o'clock   [   ] o'clock

2 Draw the hour and minute hands on the clocks to show each time.

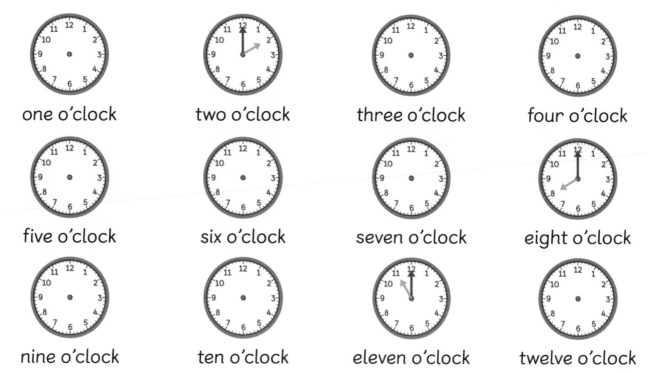

one o'clock   two o'clock   three o'clock   four o'clock

five o'clock   six o'clock   seven o'clock   eight o'clock

nine o'clock   ten o'clock   eleven o'clock   twelve o'clock

Telling time to the half hour

Starter

At what time does Hannah go to school?

We say it is half past eight.

Example

The minute hand is pointing to 6. It is half way round the clock face.

The hour hand is between 8 and 9. The hour hand has gone past 8.

The time is half past 8.

1 Write the times that these clocks show.

8:30

2 Draw the hour and minute hands on the clock faces to show each time.

half past 8

half past 9

half past 12

half past 2

half past 5

half past 6

Estimating duration of time

Starter

What can you do in 1 second?
How long is 1 minute?
How long is 1 hour?

Example

In 1 second, you can kick a ball.

In 1 minute, you can blow up a balloon.

In 1 hour, you can have a game of tennis.

Practice

Write the missing words. Use **seconds**, **minutes** or **hours**.

1. Washing the dishes takes about 20 ⬚ .

2. Going on a bike ride takes about 2 ⬚ .

3. Sneezing takes about 2 ⬚ .

4. Taking a bath takes about 30 ⬚ .

5. The school day lasts about 7 ⬚ .

Comparing time

Starter

Who is quicker?
Who is slower?

Example

Ruby and Lulu start the race at the same time.
Lulu reaches the finish line **earlier** than Ruby does.
Ruby reaches the finish line **later** than Lulu does.

Lulu is **quicker** than Ruby.
Ruby is **slower** than Lulu.

Being quicker means
taking less time.

Being slower means
taking more time.

1 Write the missing words.
Use **quicker, slower, earlier** or **later**.

(a) It is [　　　　] to take an aeroplane than a car.

(b) A tortoise is [　　　　] than a leopard.

(c) Running is [　　　　] than walking.

(d) Yesterday Hannah woke up at 7 o'clock. Today she woke up at 8 o'clock.

Hannah woke up [　　　　] today.

(e) Elliott started watching TV at 5 o'clock. Charles started watching TV at

half past 5. Elliott started watching TV [　　　　] than Charles did.

2 Write a sentence using each of these words: **quicker, slower, earlier** and **later**.

(a) _____

_____

(b) _____

_____

(c) _____

_____

(d) _____

_____

Months of the year

Starter

How many months are there in a year?

Calendar 2022

	January						
M	T	W	T	F	S	S
					1	2
3	4	5	6	7	8	9
10	11	12	13	14	15	16
17	18	19	20	21	22	23
24	25	26	27	28	29	30
31						

February						
M	T	W	T	F	S	S
	1	2	3	4	5	6
7	8	9	10	11	12	13
14	15	16	17	18	19	20
21	22	23	24	25	26	27
28						

March						
M	T	W	T	F	S	S
	1	2	3	4	5	6
7	8	9	10	11	12	13
14	15	16	17	18	19	20
21	22	23	24	25	26	27
28	29	30	31			

April						
M	T	W	T	F	S	S
				1	2	3
4	5	6	7	8	9	10
11	12	13	14	15	16	17
18	19	20	21	22	23	24
25	26	27	28	29	30	

May						
M	T	W	T	F	S	S
						1
2	3	4	5	6	7	8
9	10	11	12	13	14	15
16	17	18	19	20	21	22
23	24	25	26	27	28	29
30	31					

June						
M	T	W	T	F	S	S
		1	2	3	4	5
6	7	8	9	10	11	12
13	14	15	16	17	18	19
20	21	22	23	24	25	26
27	28	29	30			

July						
M	T	W	T	F	S	S
				1	2	3
4	5	6	7	8	9	10
11	12	13	14	15	16	17
18	19	20	21	22	23	24
25	26	27	28	29	30	31

August						
M	T	W	T	F	S	S
1	2	3	4	5	6	7
8	9	10	11	12	13	14
15	16	17	18	19	20	21
22	23	24	25	26	27	28
29	30	31				

September						
M	T	W	T	F	S	S
			1	2	3	4
5	6	7	8	9	10	11
12	13	14	15	16	17	18
19	20	21	22	23	24	25
26	27	28	29	30		

October						
M	T	W	T	F	S	S
					1	2
3	4	5	6	7	8	9
10	11	12	13	14	15	16
17	18	19	20	21	22	23
24	25	26	27	28	29	30
31						

November						
M	T	W	T	F	S	S
	1	2	3	4	5	6
7	8	9	10	11	12	13
14	15	16	17	18	19	20
21	22	23	24	25	26	27
28	29	30				

December						
M	T	W	T	F	S	S
			1	2	3	4
5	6	7	8	9	10	11
12	13	14	15	16	17	18
19	20	21	22	23	24	25
26	27	28	29	30	31	

Example

There are 12 months in a year.

January	February	March	April
May	June	July	August
September	October	November	December

In which month were you born?

There are four seasons in a year.

| spring | summer | autumn | winter |

Spring: March, April, May

Summer: June, July, August

Autumn: September, October, November

Winter: December, January, February

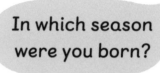 

In which season were you born?

Practice

Fill in the blanks.

1 _____ is the first month of the year.

2 There are _____ months in a year.

3 Autumn comes after _____ and before _____.

4 The three months of summer are _____ , _____ and _____ .

5 The month before August is _____ .

6 _____ is the last month of the year.

Days of the week

Starter

On which days of the week do you go to school?

October						
M	T	W	T	F	S	S
					1	2
3	4	5	6	7	8	9
10	11	12	13	14	15	16
17	18	19	20	21	22	23
24	25	26	27	28	29	30
31						

Example

The days of the week are:
Monday, Tuesday, Wednesday, Thursday, Friday, Saturday and Sunday.

Saturday and Sunday are the days of the weekend.
We don't go to school at the weekend.

Monday, Tuesday, Wednesday, Thursday, and Friday are called weekdays.
We go to school on weekdays.

Unless we're
on holiday!

26

1 Write the missing words. You can use a calendar to help you.

(a) How many days are there in a week? [ ]

(b) Which two days are the weekend?

[ ] [ ]

(c) What day comes after Thursday? [ ]

(d) What is the first day of the week? [ ]

(e) How many days a week do you go to school? [ ]

2 How many weeks are there in February? [ ]

February						
M	T	W	T	F	S	S
	1	2	3	4	5	6
7	8	9	10	11	12	13
14	15	16	17	18	19	20
21	22	23	24	25	26	27
28						

3 Do all months have the same number of whole weeks? [ ]

Recognising coins

We can use coins to pay for things.
Do you know the value of each of these coins?

These are the different coins we can use to pay for things.
Each coin is worth a different amount.

1 pence

2 pence

5 pence

10 pence

20 pence

50 pence

1 pound

2 pounds

The size and shape of a coin
does not tell us what it is worth.

28

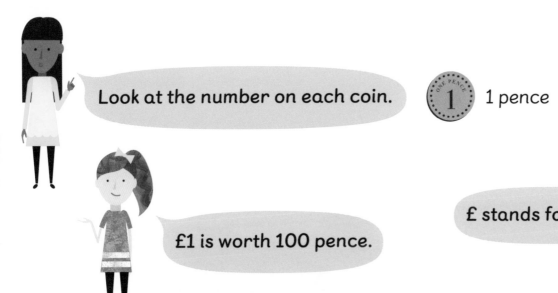

Look at the number on each coin.

1 pence

£1 1 pound

£1 is worth 100 pence.

£ stands for pound.

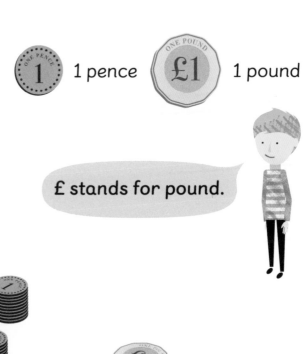

These coins both have the number 1 on them. is worth 1 pence.

£1 is worth 1 pound.

Practice

1 Circle all the 20 pence coins.

2 Circle all the 1 pound coins.

Recognising notes

Starter

How is Emma paying for her books?

Example

Emma is using a £20 note.
There are four different notes that we use.

 5 pounds

 10 pounds

 20 pounds

 50 pounds

1. What colour are the £5 notes?

   Circle all the £5 notes.

2. Which note is red?

3. Which note is worth the least?

4. Ask an adult in your home if they have a £10 note or a £20 note you can look at.

   Look at the pictures on the back of the notes. What can you see?

Comparing volume and capacity

Starter

How can we describe the amount of water in the bottles?

Example

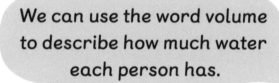

We can use the word volume to describe how much water each person has.

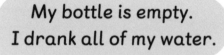

My bottle is empty. I drank all of my water.

I haven't drunk any of my water yet. My bottle is still full.

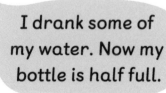

I drank some of my water. Now my bottle is half full.

Amira has a larger volume of water than Elliott and Ravi have.
Elliott has a smaller volume of water than Amira has.

1 Fill in the blanks.

Glass A

Glass B

(a) The volume of water in Glass ☐ is less than the volume of water in Glass ☐ .

The volume of water in Glass ☐ is more than the volume of water in Glass ☐ .

Glass C

Glass D

Glass E

(b) The volume of water in Glass D is more than the volume of water in Glass ☐ .

The volume of water in Glass D is less than the volume of water in Glass ☐ .

2 Colour the glasses to show the correct volume.

Glass A is full.   Glass B is empty.   Glass C is half full.

Finding volume and capacity

Starter

Which container can hold more water?

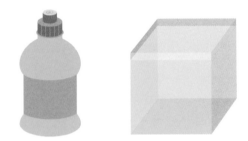

Example

We can use as a unit of measure.

It takes 4 to fill the vase.

It takes 3  to fill the water bottle.

Capacity is the most liquid the container can hold.

The vase holds more water.
It has a greater capacity than the water bottle.

1 Fill in the blanks.

The pictures show the number of glasses it takes to fill the containers.

(a)

The capacity of the jug is about ☐ glasses.

(b)

The capacity of the dog bowl is about ☐ glasses.

2 Try this at home.

Find containers in your kitchen and measure the capacity of each of them.
Count the number of glasses it takes to fill them.

Write your findings below.

Container	Capacity (number of glasses)

Describing capacity using half and quarter

Starter

How many small glasses of water will it take to fill the large glass?

Example

1

I used 2 small glasses to fill the large glass.

The capacity of one small glass is **1 half** of the capacity of the large glass.

2

It takes 4 small glasses to fill the vase.

The capacity of the small glass is **1 quarter** of the capacity of the vase.

Look at the pictures and complete the sentences with **half** or **quarter**.

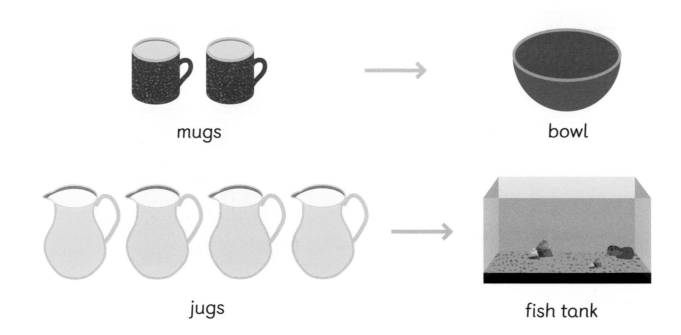

mugs

bowl

jugs

fish tank

1 After pouring 1 full mug into the bowl, the bowl is now

[   ] full.

2 After pouring 1 full jug into the fish tank, the fish tank is now a

[   ] full.

3 After pouring 2 full jugs into the fish tank, the fish tank is now

[   ] full.

Comparing the masses of objects

Starter

Can you compare the masses of these objects?

Example

I sorted the objects into two groups.

Light objects	Heavy objects

We can compare smaller objects using a balance scale.

The pineapple is **heavier** than the paintbrush.
The paintbrush is **lighter** than the pineapple.

The glue sticks and the notebook have the same mass.

1 Describe each of the following using **heavy** or **light**.

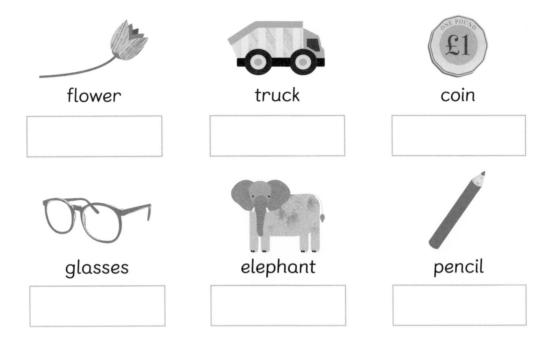

flower

truck

coin

glasses

elephant

pencil

2 Fill in the blanks.

orange

mango

(a) The [ ] is heavier than the [ ].

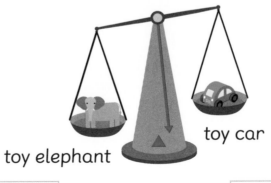

toy elephant

toy car

(b) The [ ] is lighter than the [ ].

Finding mass

Starter

How can we find the mass of the fruit?

Example

We can use 1 cube as 1 unit of mass.

We can use a balance scale to help us.

The apple has the same mass as 6 cubes.

The mass of the apple is 6 units.

Find the mass of these objects.

1 stands for 1 unit.

1

The mass of the banana is about ☐ units.

2

The grapes have the same mass as ☐ .

3

The lemon has the same mass as ☐ .

Review and challenge

1 Compare the plants using **taller**, **tallest**, **shorter** or **shortest**.

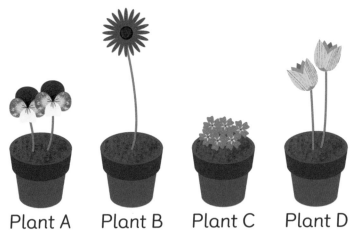

Plant A   Plant B   Plant C   Plant D

(a) Plant C is the [ ] .

(b) Plant B is the [ ] .

(c) Plant A is [ ] than Plant C.

(d) Plant A is [ ] than Plant D.

2 Measure each object using pencil sharpeners.

(a)

The chocolate bar is about [ ] long.

(b)

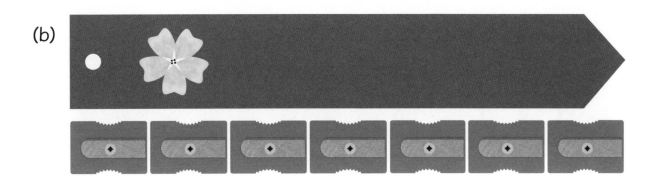

The bookmark is about [　　] 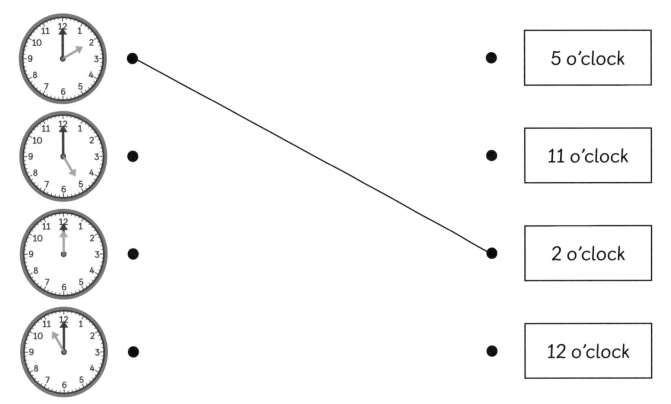 long.

3 Match the clocks with the correct times.

5 o'clock

11 o'clock

2 o'clock

12 o'clock

4 Fill in the blanks with **seconds**, **minutes** or **hours**.

(a) My journey to school takes about 30 [　　].

(b) I sleep for about 10 [　　] each day.

(c) It takes me about 5 [　　] to walk from my bedroom to the bathroom.

5 This is what Elliott does on a Sunday.

  wakes up

    cleans room

   plays football

   goes on a family outing

(a) What does Elliott do at ?

(b) What does Elliott do after he wakes up?

(c) What does Elliott do before going on a family outing?

(d) Elliott cleans his room at _____ .

6 Draw the hands on each clock to show the time.

(a)
2 o'clock

(b)
6 o'clock

(c)
8:30

(d)
half past one

7 Match each group of coins to the correct person.

Holly has the fewest 10 pence coins.

Jacob has the most 1 pound coins.

Sam has the same number of 50 pence coins as Holly has.

Holly

Jacob

Sam

8 1  stands for 1 unit.

The capacity of the goldfish bowl is [ ] units.

9 1 stands for 1 unit.

The mass of the remote control is [ ] units.

Answers

Page 5 | **1 (a)** House A is taller than House B. House B is shorter than House C. **(b)** C, A, B
2 (a) Tree A is taller than Tree B. **(b)** Tree C is shorter than Tree A. **(c)** Tree B is shorter than Tree D. **(d)** Tree D is taller than trees A, B and C. **(e)** Tree C is shorter than trees A, B and D.

Page 7 | **1 (a)** 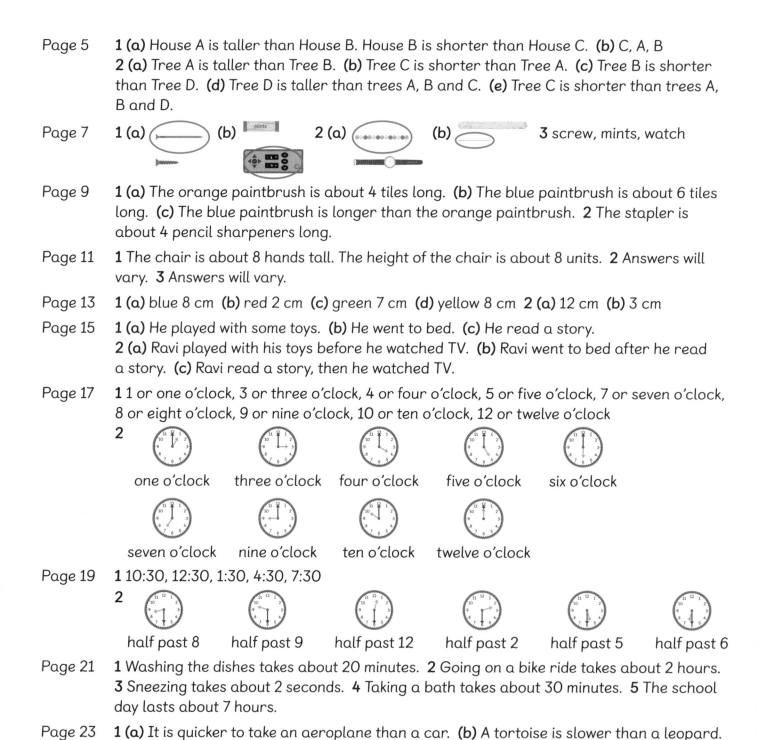 **(b)** **2 (a)** **(b)** **3** screw, mints, watch

Page 9 | **1 (a)** The orange paintbrush is about 4 tiles long. **(b)** The blue paintbrush is about 6 tiles long. **(c)** The blue paintbrush is longer than the orange paintbrush. **2** The stapler is about 4 pencil sharpeners long.

Page 11 | **1** The chair is about 8 hands tall. The height of the chair is about 8 units. **2** Answers will vary. **3** Answers will vary.

Page 13 | **1 (a)** blue 8 cm **(b)** red 2 cm **(c)** green 7 cm **(d)** yellow 8 cm **2 (a)** 12 cm **(b)** 3 cm

Page 15 | **1 (a)** He played with some toys. **(b)** He went to bed. **(c)** He read a story.
2 (a) Ravi played with his toys before he watched TV. **(b)** Ravi went to bed after he read a story. **(c)** Ravi read a story, then he watched TV.

Page 17 | **1** 1 or one o'clock, 3 or three o'clock, 4 or four o'clock, 5 or five o'clock, 7 or seven o'clock, 8 or eight o'clock, 9 or nine o'clock, 10 or ten o'clock, 12 or twelve o'clock
2

one o'clock   three o'clock   four o'clock   five o'clock   six o'clock

seven o'clock   nine o'clock   ten o'clock   twelve o'clock

Page 19 | **1** 10:30, 12:30, 1:30, 4:30, 7:30
2

half past 8   half past 9   half past 12   half past 2   half past 5   half past 6

Page 21 | **1** Washing the dishes takes about 20 minutes. **2** Going on a bike ride takes about 2 hours. **3** Sneezing takes about 2 seconds. **4** Taking a bath takes about 30 minutes. **5** The school day lasts about 7 hours.

Page 23 | **1 (a)** It is quicker to take an aeroplane than a car. **(b)** A tortoise is slower than a leopard. **(c)** Running is quicker than walking. **(d)** Hannah woke up later today. **(e)** Elliott started watching TV earlier than Charles did. **2** Answers will vary.

Page 25 | **1** January is the first month of the year. **2** There are 12 or twelve months in a year. **3** Autumn comes after summer and before winter. **4** The three months of summer are June, July and August. **5** The month before August is July. **6** December is the last month of the year.

Page 27   **1 (a)** 7 or seven **(b)** Saturday, Sunday **(c)** Friday **(d)** Monday **(e)** 5 or five **2** 4 **3** Yes

Page 29   **1**  **2**

Page 31   **1** blue or turquoise,   **2** £50 **3** £5

Page 33   **1 (a)** The volume of water in Glass B is less than the volume of water in Glass A. The volume of water in Glass A is more than the volume of water in Glass B. **(b)** The volume of water in Glass D is more than the volume of water in Glass C. The volume of water in Glass D is less than the volume of water in Glass E.

2

Page 35   **1 (a)** The capacity of the jug is about 6 glasses. **(b)** The capacity of the dog bowl is about 5 glasses. **2** Answers will vary.

Page 37   **1** After pouring 1 full mug into the bowl, the bowl is now half full. **2** After pouring 1 full jug into the fish tank, the fish tank is now a quarter full. **3** After pouring 2 full jugs into the fish tank, the fish tank is now half full.

Page 39   **1**

flower	truck	coin	glasses	elephant	pencil
light	heavy	light	light	heavy	light

2 (a) The mango is heavier than the orange. **(b)** The toy car is lighter than the toy elephant.

Page 41   **1** The mass of the banana is about 4 units. **2** The grapes have the same mass as 2 cubes. **3** The lemon has the same mass as 2 cubes.

Page 42   **1 (a)** Plant C is the shortest. **(b)** Plant B is the tallest. **(c)** Plant A is taller than Plant C. **(d)** Plant A is shorter than Plant D. **2 (a)** The chocolate bar is about 5 pencil sharpeners long.

Page 43   **(b)** The bookmark is about 7 pencil sharpeners long.

Answers continued

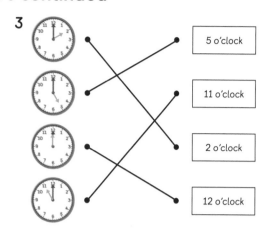

3

4 (a) My journey to school takes about 30 minutes. **(b)** I sleep for about 10 hours each day.
(c) It takes me about 5 seconds to walk from my bedroom to the bathroom.

Page 44   **5 (a)** plays football **(b)** cleans his room **(c)** plays football **(d)** 10:30

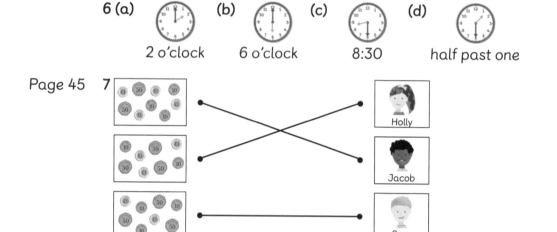

6 (a) 2 o'clock   **(b)** 6 o'clock   **(c)** 8:30   **(d)** half past one

Page 45   7

8 The capacity of the goldfish bowl is 8 units. **9** The mass of the remote control is 3 units.